The Art of Acoustic Blues Guitar

Ragtime and Gospel

Expanding repertoire and technique for fingerstyle guitar.
Featuring the music of the legendary Rev. Gary Davis.

by Woody Mann

Oak Publications
New York/London/Paris/Sydney/Copenhagen/Berlin/Tokyo/Madrid

Cover photography: © Hugh Burden/Superstock
Project editor: Ed Lozano

Order No. OK 65109
US International Standard Book Number: 0.8256.0349.8
UK International Standard Book Number: 0.7119.9685.7

Exclusive Distributors:
Music Sales Corporation
257 Park Avenue South, New York, NY 10010 USA
Music Sales Limited
8/9 Frith Street, London W1D 3JB England
Music Sales Pty. Limited
120 Rothschild Street, Rosebery, Sydney, NSW 2018, Australia

Printed in the United States of America by
Vicks Lithograph and Printing Corporation

CONTENTS

PREFACE

Welcome to the *Art of Acoustic Blues Guitar* (DVD series).

The songs presented in this series focus on the many styles and techniques used in traditional blues playing. Each lesson details the systematic procedures and approaches for performing in a particular style. These songs provide the player with the fundamental repertoire necessary in order to fully realize—through their own variations and creativity—the techniques that are applicable to the various acoustic blues styles. There are many subtleties in acoustic blues playing which can sometimes make for a confusing learning process. The goal of this series is to demonstrate a practical and simple manner for capturing the beauty of acoustic blues guitar playing. Players at every level will find the information presented in this series beneficial.

In addition, we would like to thank the many students who have attended our guitar workshops. Their feedback and progress have been indispensable in guiding the direction of this series. If you should have any questions about the music, you can contact us through our website: www.acousticsessions.com. Good luck.

Woody Mann
Trevor Laurence
Acoustic Sessions

INTRODUCTION

Ragtime and Gospel showcases the songs and techniques of two of the most fundamental and exciting styles of traditional fingerstyle guitar playing. This volume features the music of the legendary Reverend Gary Davis and presents many of his well-known songs. These songs illustrate how the music of one of the greatest guitarists can offer a complete lesson in the beauty and subtletiy of ragtime and gospel guitar playing.

Some of the ideas explored in this lesson include syncopated picking techniques, new approaches to chords and melodies, and the fundamentals of improvising within a song. The techniques covered in these tunes can be applied to a variety of musical styles and genres.

Rev. Gary Davis was one of the most gifted musicians of his generation. His music represents some of the most original and sophisticated sounds in the world of fingerstyle guitar. Developing his style from a variety of playing situations including leading church congregations, playing for dances, and performing on the streets, the Reverend's music was a unique combination of the ragtime dance feel blended with the melodic and harmonic aspects of gospel music. It was an easy choice to select the tunes for this volume as his music provides a complete lesson in fingerstyle guitar playing and the titles included showcase some of Davis' best guitar work.

I was lucky enough to study privately with the Reverend and, in this volume, I teach six of his ragtime and gospel tunes just as Davis taught me—slowly and note-for-note. Each song is presented in its basic form along with demonstrations of the way Davis played countless variations and improvisations within the piece. Guitarists with only a basic background in fingerpicking, as well as more advanced players, will benefit from these beautiful and exciting arrangements.
This is an in-depth lesson in two of the most exciting styles of acoustic blues guitar as well as a rare look into the music of one of the true original masters of ragtime and gospel music.

A Note on the Fingerpicking

An understanding of basic fingerpicking techniques is helpful to play the songs in the *Art of Acoustic Blues Guitar* series. Even though there are chords, riffs, and melodies that are unique to each tune there is a common idea in the picking approach that will enable you to see a connection between all the songs.

This fingerstyle picking is basically a two-line idea. The bass line is played with the thumb, and the treble line is played with the fingers. The goal is to develop an independence of the two parts. The greater the independence, the easier it becomes to negotiate the rhythm and syncopation, and capture the subtleties of the music. We'll then have the foundation to add many other idiomatic blues guitar techniques, such as, damping, bending, brushing, snapping the strings, *etc.*

Many of the traditional acoustic blues guitar styles were developed by guitarists imitating the two-handed approach of the piano. Just as the pianist learns to play different parts with each hand, the fingerstyle guitarist must learn to play with the thumb and fingers of the picking hand.

To illustrate the individual lines, the music is written with double stems: up stems for the melody (played with the fingers) and down stems for the bass (played with the thumb).

Developing this technique is a natural step-by-step process. At first, the goal is to play a simple bass on the beat with your thumb while playing a simple melody with your fingers. The next step is to embellish both parts with rhythmic syncopations and melodic variations. The songs featured in this series demonstrate this development—each lesson includes tunes with a simple bass and melody part as well as songs that have more complex picking. It is a good idea to play the songs slowly and keep this two-line idea in mind as you progress through the DVD.

As an example, I have written out a typical twelve-bar ragtime blues verse four different ways. The examples demonstrate some of the methods the melody and bass play off each other and how they can be embellished, along with chords, to create variations.

In *Example 1*, the bass is alternating on the beat while a simple melody line is played on top. Notice that in *Example 2* the bass remains steady while the melody becomes more rhythmic. Next, *Example 3* further develops the rhythmic movement in the bass as well as the melody. Notice the interaction between the two voices: In measures 9 and 10, the bass line has a slightly more syncopated feel and with the use of thumb rolls creates more melodic movement. And finally, *Example 4* uses more syncopation, riffs, and broken chords in both parts to create a completely different sounding guitar part from the first example.

This is a brief overview of the picking technique. The lessons in this series go into greater detail and explain, step-by-step, how to achieve this. Developing a good sound and being able to create variations in your playing begins with having a relaxed and strong picking hand. As Gary Davis use to say (about the great ragtime guitarist Blind Blake), "Now *he's* got a sportin' thumb."

Woody Mann

EXAMPLE ONE

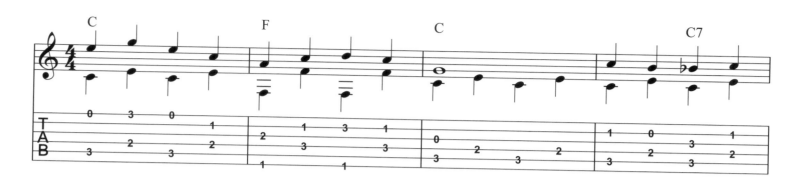

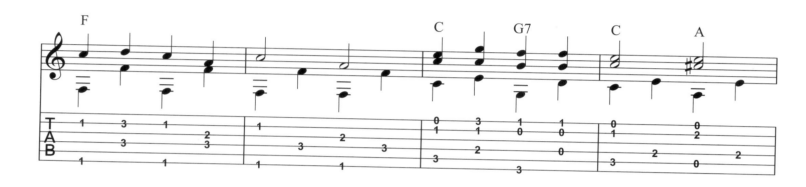

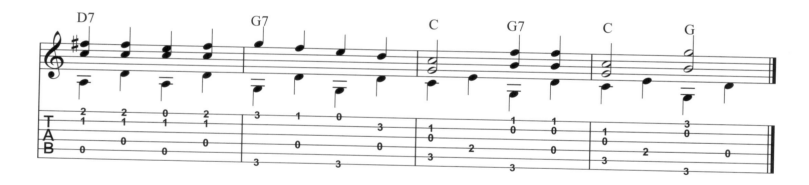

Example Two

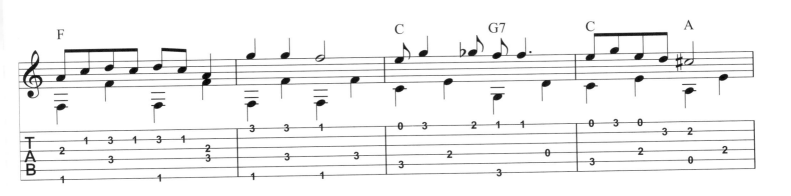

EXAMPLE THREE

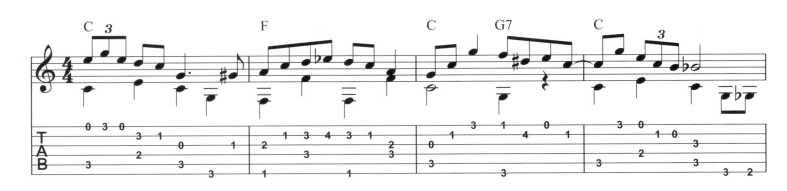

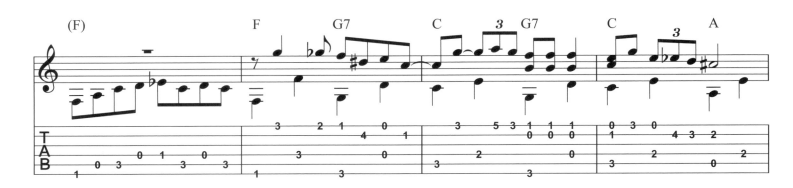

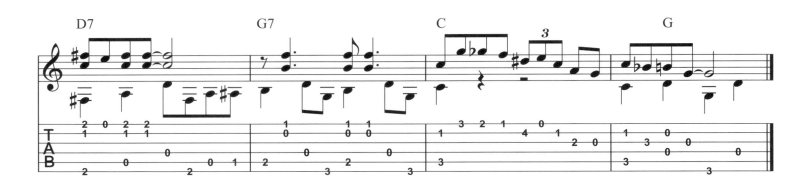

EXAMPLE FOUR

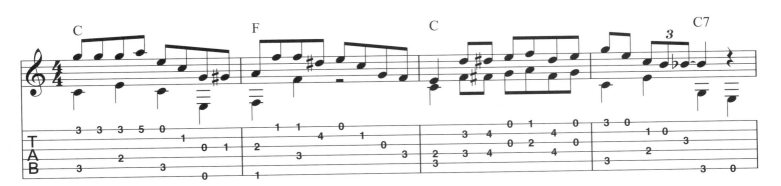

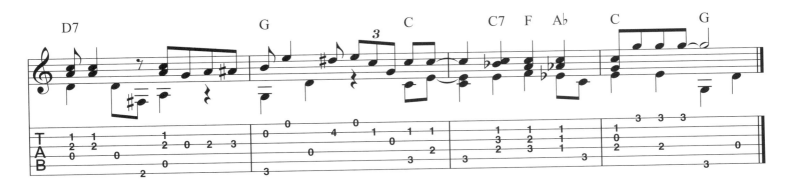

O Glory

DEATH DON'T HAVE NO MERCY

LET US GET TOGETHER

Break (High Part)

Hesitation Blues

Verse 2

Verse 3

Verse 4

I Am the Light of This World

Chorus

MAKE BELIEVE STUNT